STONE AGE SCIENCE

MATERIALS

Inventions that changed the world—and the science behind them

WRITTEN BY FELICIA LAW & GERRY BAILEY
ILLUSTRATED BY MIKE PHILLIPS

Crabtree Publishing Company
www.crabtreebooks.com
1-800-387-7650

Published in Canada
616 Welland Ave.
St. Catharines, ON
L2M 5V6

Published in the United States
PMB 59051, 350 Fifth Ave.
59th Floor,
New York, NY 10118

Authors: Felicia Law and Gerry Bailey
Illustrators: Mike Phillips, Henu Studio
Editors: Shirley Duke, Kelly Spence
Proofreader: Wendy Scavuzzo
Production coordinator and
Prepress technician: Tammy McGarr
Print coordinator: Margaret Amy Salter

Photo credits:
Cover & p1- David M. Schrader
p6 top- Dmitry Zimin; middle- Astudio; bottom- Kuznetcov Konstantin
p9 top- Mitrofanov Alexander; middle- Veniamin Kraskov; bottom- Gary L Jones
p10 top- Tanewpix ; middle- Peter Gaudella; bottom- Pulen
p14 top- ZMKStudio; middle- Andrew Bassett; bottom- Matee Nuserm
p18 top- TFoxFoto; bottom- Kateryna Zakorko
p22 top- Photo Fun; middle- Eldad Carin; bottom- pic Minahil Sherazi p24 top- Pavel Kosak; middle- Marcel Clemens; bottom- hxdyl;
base- Everett Historical
p28 top- Anton Petrus; middle- mehmetcan; bottom- Joanna Stankiewicz - Wite

Printed in the USA/082015/SN20150529

Library and Archives Canada Cataloguing in Publication

Law, Felicia, author
Stone age science : Materials / Felicia Law, Gerry Bailey ; Mike Phillips, illustrator.

(Stone Age science)
Includes index.
Issued in print and electronic formats.
ISBN 978-0-7787-1889-5 (bound).--ISBN 978-0-7787-1915-1 (paperback).--
ISBN 978-1-4271-1678-9 (pdf).--ISBN 978-1-4271-1674-1 (html)

1. Materials--Juvenile literature. I. Bailey, Gerry, 1945-, author
II. Phillips, Mike, 1961-, illustrator III. Title.

TA403.2.L4 2015 j620.1'1 C2015-903160-5
C2015-903161-3

Library of Congress Cataloging-in-Publication Data

Law, Felicia, author.
Stone age science : materials / Felicia Law & Gerry Bailey ; Illustrated by Mike Phillips.
pages cm. -- (Stone age science)
Includes index.
ISBN 978-0-7787-1889-5 (reinforced library binding) --
ISBN 978-0-7787-1915-1 (pbk.) -- ISBN 978-1-4271-1678-9 (electronic pdf)
-- ISBN 978-1-4271-1674-1 (electronic html)
1. Materials--Juvenile literature. 2. Materials science--Juvenile literature.
I. Bailey, Gerry, 1945- author. II. Phillips, Mike, 1961- illustrator. III. Title.

TA403.2.L39 2016
620.1'1--dc23

2015019153

CONTENTS

MEET LEO

Meet Leo, the brightest kid on the block.

So that's Leo!

Bright as in IQ off the scale, inventive as in Leonardo da Vinci inventive, and way, way ahead of his time...

Block as in Stone Age block. Stone Age as in 30,000 years ago.

Then there's Pallas—Leo's pet.

Pallas is wild. His ancestors have been around for millions of years. You won't see many Pallas cats around today, unless you happen to be visiting the icy, cold wasteland of Arctic Siberia in northern Russia.

And there's a cast of other characters who are all inventors—sort of!

PAINT

Leo and Pallas are spending the afternoon at an art exhibit. Leo has plenty to say about the paintings. Pallas doesn't have an opinion about art—any kind of art—which is why Leo is taking so long to explain the paintings to him.

"You see, Pallas, it's sort of modern and old at the same time. It's full of movement, but it's motionless, too. It's bright, but it's dull. I think it's a painting that..."

Leo goes on and on...and on.

Soon, it's time to leave. Leo thinks he could paint much better pictures himself. He just needs paint.

PALLAS SUGGESTS...

- *Pallas digs lots of holes. When the holes fill up with rain, they become mud puddles. Leo can make some mud paint!*
- *He can also make red powder out of red beetles—once they're dead of course!*

Paint is the substance artists use to make a picture. Paint is spread on a surface such as canvas, wood, paper, or even stone. Paints are made by mixing dry, powdered colors called **pigments** with sticky substances called **binders**.

When a sticky binder dries out and hardens, it holds the colored pigment to the surface. Modern pigments come from soil that has been colored by **minerals** such as **iron**, or from materials made in a factory.

There are many kinds of binders. Some are made from sticky vegetable gums such as gum arabic, a natural gum made of hardened sap, or vegetable oils such as linseed oil. Egg yolks are also used as binders.

Different binders dry at different speeds. This affects the shine or texture of a painting. Adding an oil-based liquid such as turpentine can thin out paint.

PIGMENTS AND BINDERS

The first pigments came from crushed soft rocks or soil that was colored by minerals. Minerals are naturally-occuring solids that are found in the ground.

Powdered pigments on sale in a Morroccan market.

Minerals such as clay and ocher, a kind of iron ore, produce reds, yellows, and browns. Charcoal can be used to make black. The mineral copper oxide can be crushed to make the color green.

Pigments can be mixed with water to form dyes.

There are different kinds of paints for different coloring jobs. Watercolors are thin, transparent paints for use on paper. Acrylics, made of pigment and a binder, are thick and easy to use when painting on a canvas. They dry quickly and turn into plastic. Oils are the thickest paints and can take days to dry. An artist can easily make many changes before the paint dries. Unfortunately, oils are expensive and messy, and you can't use water to clean them up.

An artist mixes oil paints on a palette to get the shades that are needed.

PRINT A T-SHIRT

You will need

- ***two large potatoes***
- ***a sharp knife***
- ***fabric paint***
- ***a paintbrush***
- ***a white T-shirt***

1. ***Carefully cut the potatoes in half.***

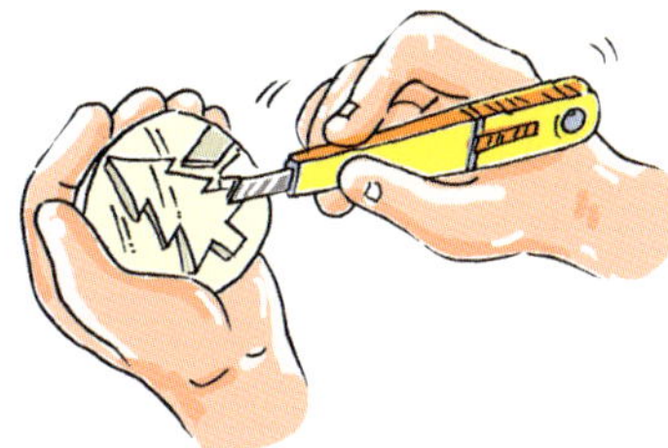

2. ***Use the knife to carve simple shapes onto each potato half.***

3. ***Carefully cut away the potato from around the design to create a stamp.***

4. ***Paint each stamp with a different color of fabric paint.***

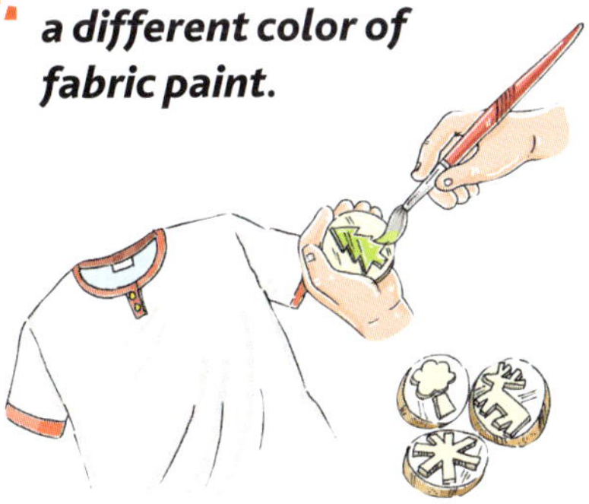

5. ***Press the potato stamps on the T-shirt to print a pattern.***

TRY PRINTING YOUR OWN GREETING CARDS AND WRAPPING PAPER, TOO!

THE CANNON

It's the start of spring vacation, and there's going to be a party. Leo wants to wake everyone up from their winter sleep—with a flash and a bang! He lights a sparkler, and although it makes lots of flashing sparks, it doesn't make much of a bang.

"I need to light a huge pile of sparklers at the same time," he says.

Pallas thinks it sounds too dangerous.

A **cannon** is a large gun with a diameter of at least 1 inch (2.5 cm). Usually, it is fitted to a **carriage** made of wood so it can be easily moved. Cannons are artillery, or weapons, that fire cannon balls.

The first cannons may have been invented in China, but they were used in Europe from about 1350. Most cannons were made of bronze or wrought iron—a kind of iron that can be shaped.

The first cannonballs were made of iron and weighed over 661 pounds (300 kg). Later, they were made from stone, or stone covered with lead. The explosion from a cannon could shoot a ball more than 1 mile (1.6 km).

GUNPOWDER

When substances burn, they often change into something else. Substances such as **gunpowder** burn very quickly. As it burns, gunpowder turns into a high-pressure gas. This means the gas quickly **expands**, or gets bigger. Substances that do this are called **explosives**.

The explosion of early gunpowder created clouds of smoke on the battlefield.

The first kind of gunpowder was called black powder. It was made of sulfur, charcoal, and **saltpeter**. Saltpeter is a white powder found in soil that is used in fertilizers, medicine, and gunpowder. The three ingredients were pressed together and broken into small pieces, or used as a powder.

Gunpowder is the explosive force behind colorful fireworks.

In a cannon, gunpowder is packed into the weapon's **tube**. The tube is open at one end. The cannon is aimed at its target using its **chassis**, or frame. Once the powder is set on fire, the expanding gas shoots an object, such as a cannonball, out of the tube at high speed. Ready, aim, fire!

RUBBER

Bounce, bounce, bounce! Leo has discovered a stretchy substance called rubber. He has also discovered that a ball of rubber will bounce. There are lots of things he can do with this new material—but first he's going to play!

The sap of the rubber tree is collected in cups.

Rubber is made from the gummy sap of the rubber tree. A white, milky liquid called **latex** runs through small veins in the tree's bark. The latex is collected by **tapping**, which is the process of making a cut in the tree, and inserting a small tube. The latex oozes out into a bucket.

After the latex is collected, it must be softened. It is passed between large rollers, then mixed with chemicals to strengthen and stiffen it. Next, the latex is pressed into large sheets. These sheets are cut, shaped, and exported as rubber to places all over the world.

Rubber tires are found on most vehicles.

Stretchy rubber bands hold things tightly together.

MAKE RUBBER MUSIC

You will need
- *paint*
- *a paintbrush*
- *a cardboard tube*
- *glitter*
- *sequins*
- *rubber bands*
- *scissors*
- *glue*

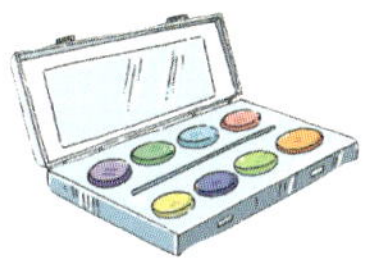

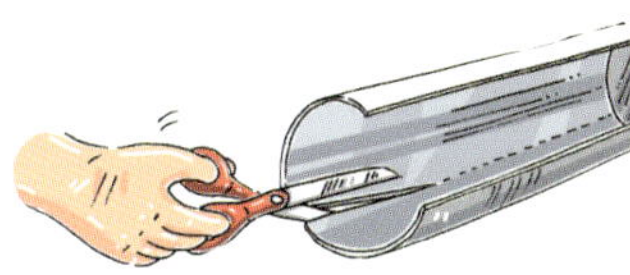

1. *Cut the sides off the cardboard tube, leaving the circular base.*

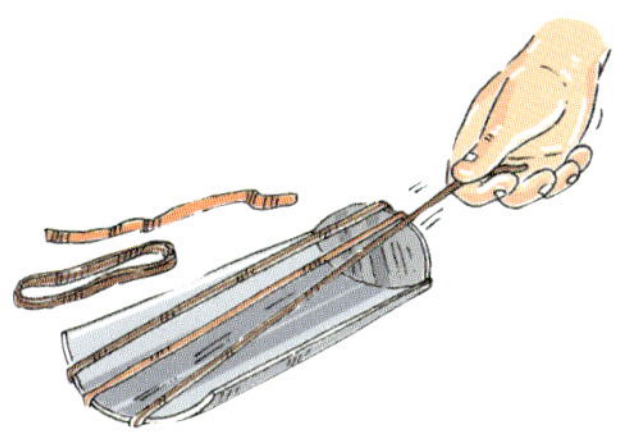

2. *Glue pieces of rubber bands from one end to the other.*

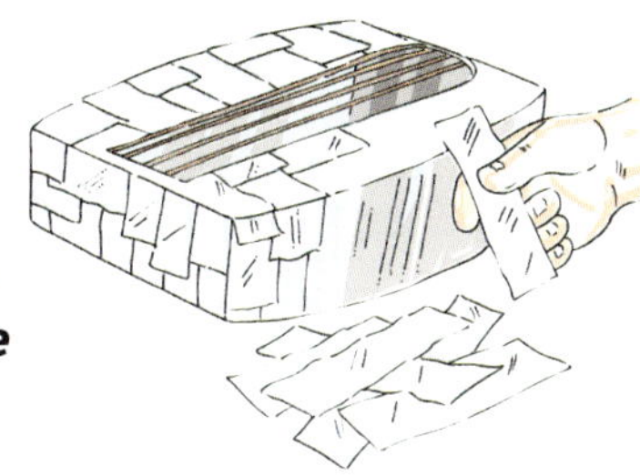

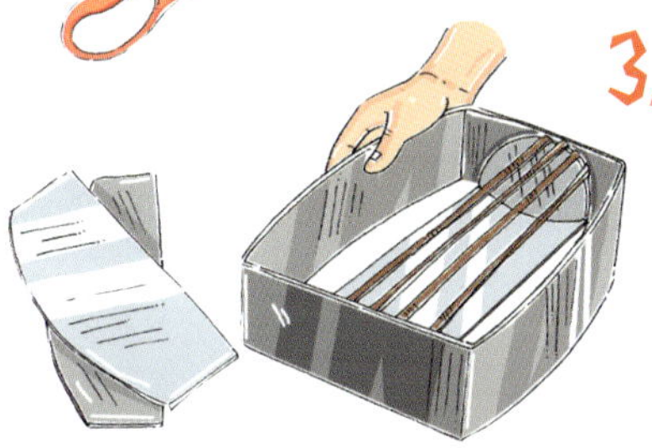

3. *Make a frame from an empty tissue box. Glue the tube inside.*

4. *Glue on strips of newspaper or other colored paper.*

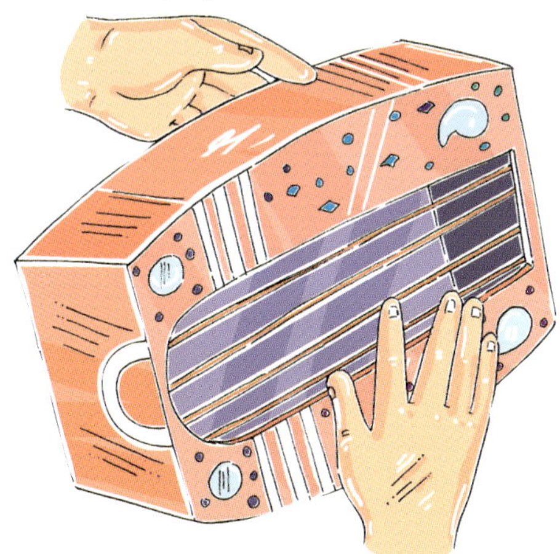

5. *When the glue dries, paint the box a bright color and decorate it with sequins and glitter.*

PLUCK THE STRINGS AND MAKE MUSIC!

ARMOR

It's time to collect the honey from the honeycombs! However the bees are fiercely protecting their hive. They won't let Leo and Pallas near the honeycombs.

"I don't want to get stung," says Leo. Pallas agrees. He doesn't want to get stung, either!

Unfortunately, their beekeeper's masks only cover a small part of their bodies. There are lots of places where the bees can still attack. They need more protection.

PALLAS SUGGESTS...

- *They could make a shield to hold in front of their bodies. Of course, the bees could just fly around the shield.*

- *They could wrap their whole bodies in skins so the bees could not reach their skin.*

Plate armor was developed in Europe during the 1300s. It was needed to protect soldiers because **chain mail**, or armor made up of tiny rings of metal linked together, could be pierced by crossbow arrows or crushed by other weapons. Plate armor covered the entire body with large pieces of steel.

The suit, worn by a knight, included a helmet, breastplate, **gauntlets**, or gloves, and shoes called **sollerets**. Even the knight's horse wore plate armor. Although it offered good protection, plate armor was heavy, hot, and very expensive to make.

Later, armor was fashionably decorated for parades and tournaments. It was sometimes etched with silver or gold. Still, even strong plate armor could not protect against new weapons that used gunpowder. So, by the late 1500s, it was no longer used.

STEEL

Steel is made from iron. Iron is an **element** which is **extracted** from iron ore—rock that contains iron. To extract the iron, the ore is heated with limestone and **coke**, which is made from coal. The limestone and coke remove oxygen from the ore, leaving behind mostly pure iron. This process is called **smelting**.

Molten metal, or metal melted by heat, is poured into a mold and left to cool until it sets into a solid shape.

Today, most factories use an **oxygen furnace** to make steel. This process is about ten times faster. In an oxygen furnace, after iron has been melted at a high temperature, purified oxygen is blown into the molten metal. The oxygen reacts with unwanted elements and removes them. At this stage, other elements are added to the iron.

When the metal is cool, it can be rolled and pressed into sheets.

An **alloy** is a mixture of one metal with another element. Creating an alloy can create stronger, harder, and tougher materials. Common steel alloys contain iron, **carbon**, and other metals. **Stainless steel** is a steel alloy which does not rust. It is made by adding the element chromium to steel.

These rolls of steel will be used to make products in factories.

MAKE A PLUMED HELMET

You will need

- a felt tip pen
- a large balloon
- strips of newspaper
- white glue
- scissors
- cardboard
- a string
- feathers
- double-sided tape
- index cards
- thin wire
- a stapler and staples
- paint and a paintbrush

1. Draw a helmet shape on an inflated balloon and cover it with layers of newspaper soaked in a mixture of half glue and half water. When the newspaper is dry, pop the balloon.

2. Cut out a visor, earflaps, and a strip from the cardboard. Glue on the strip and use string to decorate it.

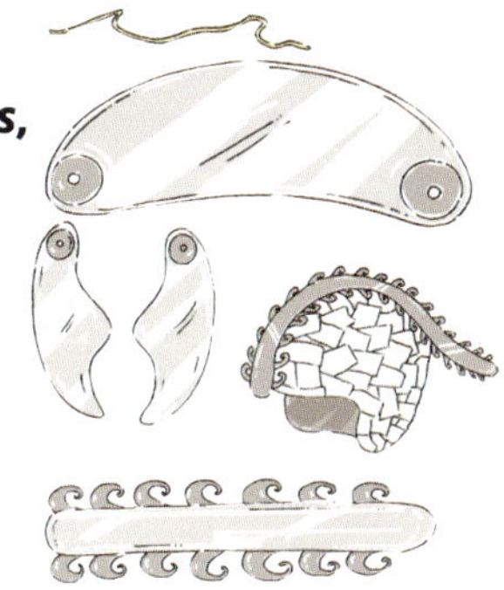

3. Attach the feathers to a strip of cardboard covered with tape, then form the cardboard into a circle. Decorate the base with string.

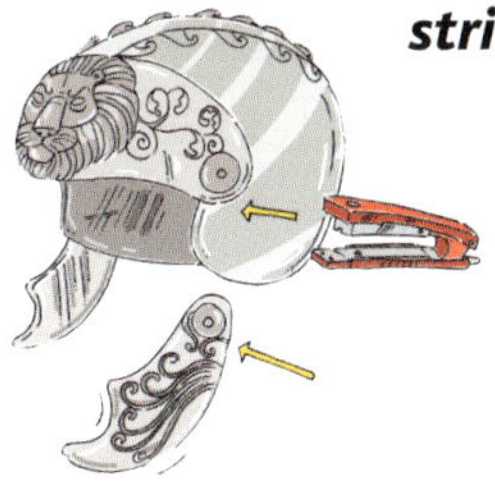

4. To build the helmet, tape card hinges to the earflaps. Make holes in each side of the helmet, then thread the wire through the hinges and helmet. Twist the wires together on the inside and cover the ends with tape so they won't scratch you. Staple on the visor.

5. Attach the plume to the helmet, then paint!

CONCRETE

"Okay!" says Leo. "There's work to do! And everyone has to help out."

Leo decides that they are going to build something. They could build a shed, a jungle gym for the children, or a flagpole for the villagers. But whatever they build, it will need to stand on a strong foundation. Without a strong base, it might sink into the ground or be washed away in a storm.

No one is exactly sure what a strong foundation is, although it doesn't sound very exciting—and if they DID know, they would probably all say they were too busy to help!

PALLAS SUGGESTS...

- *Leo could use his cakes to build the base that's needed. They're pretty strong. In fact, his cakes are as hard as any rock!*

- *Another idea is that he could grind up some rocks. After all, rocks are strong.*

Concrete is a type of artificial stone made by mixing dry sand or gravel and **cement**, then adding water. This makes a soft mixture that can be formed into different shapes.

Concrete is made stronger by increasing the cement and reducing the other ingredients. It takes several days for wet concrete to **set**, or harden, properly.

Concrete gets stronger as time passes. In fact, it continues strengthening for about five years after it sets! This process is called **curing**.

Concrete was discovered in the floor of a Stone Age village in the former Yugoslavia, built around 5600 BCE. It was also used in bridges and aqueducts built by the Romans around 200 BCE.

STRENGTH & RESISTANCE

Scientists and engineers look at the strength and toughness of a material to determine the best way to use it. There are different kinds of strength, and not all materials are strong in the same way. Some materials have **compression** strength. This means they can be **compressed**, or squeezed.

A ball has compression strength because it can be squeezed and pressed but it doesn't burst.

Cement is a tough material used to lay foundations and build walls.

Other materials have **tensile strength**. This means they can be pulled apart. A length of rope has tensile strength because you can tug on it and it will take a lot of pulling before it snaps.

Reinforced concrete slabs and pillars are used to create a strong frame for this building.

Some materials are simply tough. They can take a lot of pulling, pushing, and hard use before they break or pull apart. Most materials used in buildings have this kind of tough strength. **Reinforced concrete**, or concrete strengthened by steel bars, is stronger than either material by itself.

TESTING MATERIALS

You will need
- modeling clay
- straw
- sand
- strong thread
- a plastic cup
- kitchen scales
- scissors
- pebbles
- a sharp knife
- a ruler

1. Break off three pieces of clay. With the knife and ruler, shape one piece into a brick approximately 4 inches (10 cm) long, 2 inches (5 cm) wide, and 1 inch (2.5 cm) high.

2. Cut five or six pieces of straw about 4 inches (10 cm) long. Work these into the second piece of clay, then make another brick.

3. Finally, mix three pinches of sand into the third piece of clay, then form a third brick.

Leave all three bricks to harden overnight.

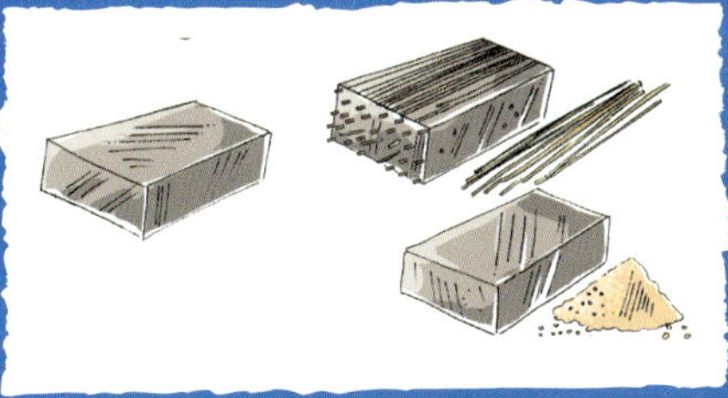

4. Make two piles of books about 16 inches (40 cm) tall on either side of the bowl. Next, make two small holes in the top of the plastic cup and insert the thread. Tie the thread in a loop about 24 inches (60 cm) long. Place the loop over the middle of the first brick, then set the brick between the two piles of books.

5. Slowly pour pebbles into the cup until the thread snaps under the weight. Pour the pebbles back into the cup and weigh them on the scale. Record your measurements.

Repeat the experiment with the other two bricks.

WHAT DO YOU NOTICE?

THE CAMERA

Leo is packing his suitcase. He's going on vacation and it's time to say goodbye to all of his friends.
"OK! Goodbye!" they all say.

"Wait," says Leo. "Won't you miss me? I'll be gone for two whole weeks."
"Okay," they say. "Have a great time."

"Hey!" says Leo. "How will I have a great time when I'm missing all of my friends? I feel sad already. I don't know what I'll do without you. Maybe you should all go and pack—then you can come, too!"

Pallas was looking forward to a vacation, too—at last, a break from Leo's inventions and all that hard work! He needs to come up with an idea—and fast—so Leo will not miss his friends.

PALLAS SUGGESTS...

- *Maybe Leo could make small models of us and carry them in a box.*

- *Or he could paint a picture of everyone...but that would take a long time. Leo really needs some kind of instant picture!*

A camera is a device for taking photographs. Light passes through one or more **lenses** then onto a film coated with silver-based **crystals**. These crystals make the film sensitive to light.

When a picture is taken, the crystals on the film change, depending on how much light hits them. This makes a **negative** picture, with the dark and light parts reversed. The film is then developed to produce a **positive** image that looks like the object the camera photographed.

Color film has three layers of light-sensitive chemicals. Each one is sensitive to a different color. These three colors combine to form a life-like color photo.

Today, digital cameras can take pictures and transfer them to a computer or tablet in seconds.

CRYSTALS

Most minerals occur naturally as crystals. A crystal is a solid material with a natural geometric shape. A crystal of sugar, for example, looks like a tiny cube. A quartz crystal is a **hexagonal**, or six-sided, shape. Crystals of different substances have different shapes. Crystals are often hard and shiny, and have smooth, flat surfaces.

Crystals come in many different shapes and colors.

Silver is mixed with other chemicals and used to coat photographic film. When the film is exposed to light in the camera, the crystals in the mixture change to produce an image of the object the camera is photographing.

An early pinhole camera.

A **pinhole camera** is a simple camera that can take pictures. In a pinhole camera, a tiny hole replaces the lens. Light travels through the pinhole and produces an **inverted**, or upside down, image on a viewing screen.

This negative picture was taken using a pinhole camera made from a can. The inside of the can was painted black so no light could enter. The hole was covered with a piece of aluminum foil, and light-sensitive photo paper was placed inside the can.

MAKE A PINHOLE CAMERA

You will need

- ***a small cardboard box, or a piece of cardboard to make your own box***
- ***a thin plastic lid or piece of thin index card***
- ***a thumbtack***
- ***a sheet of wax paper***
- ***tape***
- ***glue***
- ***paint***

1. ***If you cannot find the right-sized box, you can make one by folding and gluing cardboard. Leave the box open at one end.***

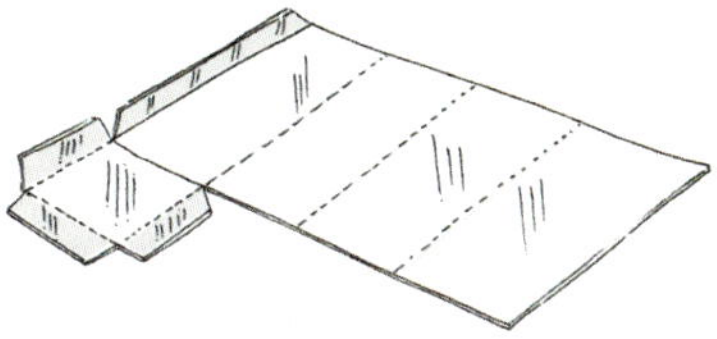

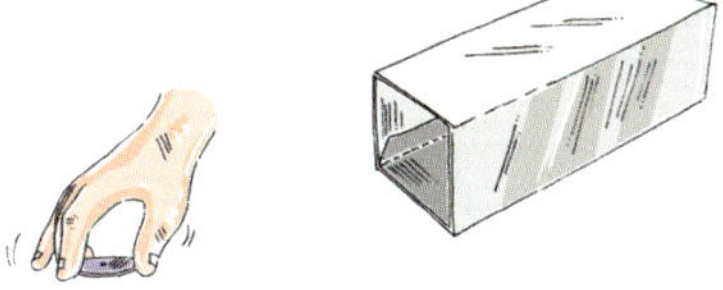

2. ***At the closed end, cut a hole smaller than the plastic lid. This is where the lens will be.***

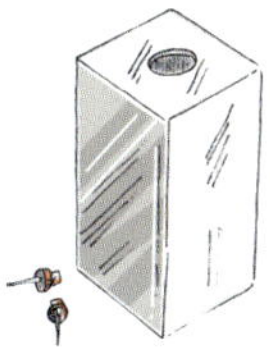

3. ***Make a hole in the plastic lid with the thumbtack, then glue the lid over the hole.***

4. ***Stretch and tape a piece of wax paper tightly over the open end of the box to make your viewing screen.***

5. ***Fold and glue a piece of index card around the camera so that the screen is well shaded, then glue it to the camera. Paint and decorate your camera.***

6. ***Look through the tiny hole. What do you see?***

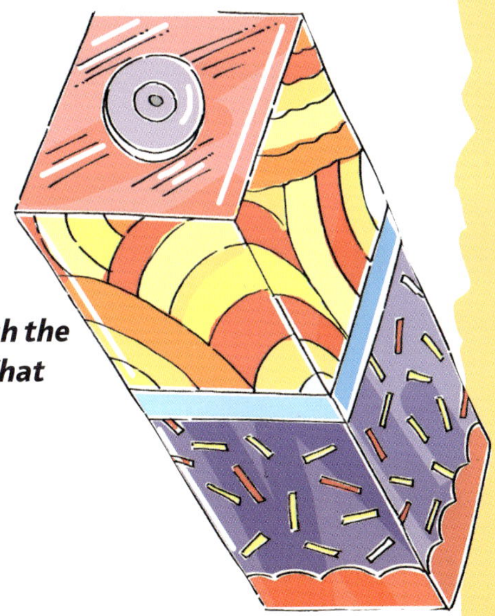

MARIE CURIE

A MAMMOTH INVENTOR!

Marie Sklodowska was born in Poland in 1867. She was a good student and won a gold medal for achievement when she finished high school. Marie decided to become a teacher.

After finishing school at a university in Paris, Marie began work in a research laboratory. There, she met Pierre Curie. They got married in 1895 and began a famous partnership.

Marie became very interested in mysterious rays. These invisible signals were rays coming from a rock made up of different substances called **pitchblende**.

After many experiments, Marie and Pierre found the element. It gave off such strong rays that it glowed in the dark. They named it **radium**.

URANIUM

Marie and Pierre Curie's greatest scientific discovery was finding two elements: polonium and radium. This discovery led to the invention of X-ray technology and **nuclear energy**.

The Curies knew that uranium gave off a strange kind of energy in the form of rays. Marie later called this energy **radiation**. But they were determined to find other sources.

They found that thorium, another element, was **radioactive**. Even more important, they found strong radioactivity in pitchblende. They performed experiments breaking down the pitchblende to find out where the radiation was coming from. Marie discovered that radium was the source. Sadly, she died from coming in contact with it for so long.

Marie Curie lived from 1867 to1934. Both she and her husband were **physicists**. In 1904, they were awarded the Nobel Prize in chemistry. Marie became the first woman to ever win the Nobel Prize. She was awarded a second Nobel Prize in physics in 1911.

A machine drills for uranium deep inside a mine.

Uranium rock, from which radium can be obtained.

Radioactive material is removed from uranium in a power station to make nuclear energy.

GLASS

It's been raining all day. Leo and Pallas huddle inside their cave and try to stay warm. However, the rain keeps pouring in through all the open windows. Leo and Pallas are soaked!

Leo could hang skins over the windows, but then it would be dark inside the cave.

He needs to figure out a way to cover the windows that will keep them dry, but also let in light. A transparent, or clear, material would be ideal.

PALLAS SUGGESTS...

- *If Leo lit a fire, he could heat some sugar so that it reached its melting point and changed from a solid to a liquid. When it cools, it hardens into clear, see-through toffee.*
- *Perhaps Leo could do the same thing with sand. After all, it looks like sugar.*

Glass is a hard, clear substance made from three minerals: sand, soda, and lime. Soda comes from a combination of two elements. These minerals are heated to a very high temperature until they **fuse**, or melt together. This process, known as **fusion**, makes glass.

Glass was first used to make small pots, vases, and jugs. A glassblower collected a small blob of glowing, hot glass on the end of a long pipe. Then, he or she skillfully shaped it into a jug or vase by spinning it around, while at the same time blowing air through the pipe to create a hollow center. After the liquid glass had been shaped, it had to cool slowly. This process is known as **annealing**.

Flat glass was first made by blowing a bubble of molten glass, then spinning it until it was flat. This created small sheets of glass with a little bump in the middle, which is known as **crown glass**. The flat glass around the bump was cut into window panes.

MELTING POINT

A **melting point** is the temperature at which a substance changes from a solid to a liquid. Different solids have different melting points. For example, the melting point of ice is 32°F (0°C). The melting point of steel is much higher—about 2,732°F (1,500°C).

Any substance will melt if it is heated to its own specific melting point. Mixtures of substances melt over a range of temperatures, depending on what they contain.

Mixtures such as glass, made up of sand, soda, and lime, do not simply melt—they also become softer as their temperature increases.

Glass can be heated until it becomes sticky like caramel and easy to work with.

Glass can be colored with pigments to make stained glass windows with bright colors.

Glassblowers carefully shape the hot blob of glass on the ends of the pipes.

Glass comes in many shapes and colors.

DESIGN A STAINED GLASS WINDOW

You will need

- *a white pencil*
- *a black posterboard or heavy black paper*
- *scissors or a craft knife*
- *colored tissue paper*
- *glue*
- *tape*

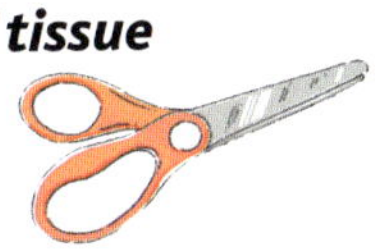

1. *With a white pencil, draw patterns on a piece of black posterboard or paper.*

2. *Carefully cut out the shapes, leaving a frame around each one.*

3. *Turn the frame over, so you're working on the back. Glue pieces of colored tissue paper across the spaces.*

4. *Tape your pattern to a window so that light shines through.*

STAINED GLASS WINDOWS WERE USED TO TELL A STORY, AS WELL AS TO LET IN LIGHT.

MAKE CRYSTALS

You will need
- piece of thread
- salt
- glass of hot water
- pencil
- measuring cup

1. Pour 3 ounces (100 ml) of hot water into the glass. Add 4 teaspoons (20 ml) of salt. Mix well until all the salt has dissolved.

2.

Tie the thread around the middle of the pencil. Place this on the glass so that the thread reaches the water. Make sure the thread is under the water.

3. Salt crystals will start to form on the string in a few days. You can make the crystals larger if you change the water each day with fresh salt water.

SPOON DROP TEST

You will need
- a large plastic container
- 8 x 8 inch (20 x 20 cm) squares of: newspaper, plastic wrap, aluminum foil, and wax paper
- roll of masking tape
- thick rubber band
- meter stick
- metal spoon

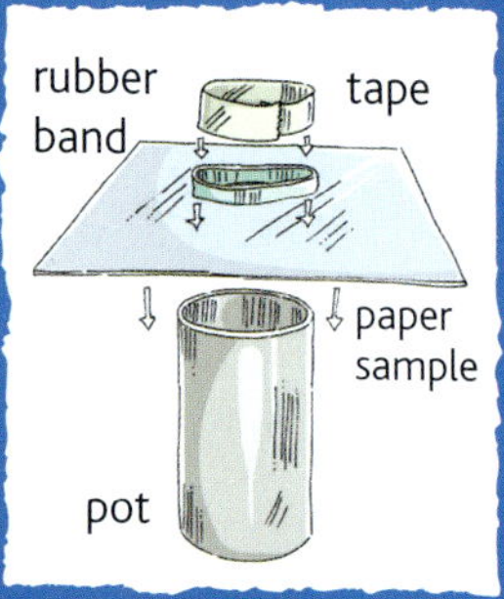

1. Select one of the paper samples. Place it over the top of the pot and fasten with a rubber band. Secure the rubber band with tape.

2. Hold the covered container next to the meter stick. Hold the spoon by its handle, with the bottom of the spoon about 5 inches (13 cm) above the top of the pot. Now drop the spoon straight down on the paper sample. Does the paper dent or break?

If not, keep increasing the distance of the drop by 2 inches (5 cm) until the paper breaks. Repeat the test with all four kinds of paper.

3. Record your findings in a chart. Which paper was the strongest? Which was the weakest?

GLOSSARY

Note: Some boldfaced words are defined where they appear in the book.

alloy A solid substance made by melting a metal and adding in smaller amounts of other metals and non-metals

carbon Carbon is an element found in all living things

carriage A wheeled structure that is used to carry and move something heavy

cement A powdery mixture of clay and lime that sets when water is added

crystal A solid material with a flat face and sharp angles. Many crystal rocks form when melted rock in Earth's crust cools and hardens

element A solid, liquid, or gas made of the same kind of atoms; everything in the world is made up of elements that join together in different ways

extracted Removed from

fusion The process of substances melting and joining to make new substances

gunpowder Gunpowder is a compound that explodes when heated

iron A heavy metallic mineral that rusts easily

lenses Transparent, curved pieces of glass or plastic used in items such as eyeglasses and cameras to make things look clearer, smaller, or bigger

mineral A substance that forms naturally in the ground

negative An image on film in which the lightest areas of the photograph are the darkest and the darkest areas are the lightest

nuclear energy The energy released during nuclear fission or fusion, especially when used to generate electricity

physicists Scientists who study the science of matter, energy, and their interactions

pitchblende The ore of the element uranium

positive A film that recreates an original image in tone and color, unlike a negative in which colors appear reversed

radioactive Describing what happens when some elements break down and give off different kinds of energy

smelting A process that involves melting metals at a high temperature to soften them to be formed into different shapes

tensile strength The amount something can stretch, or be stretched, without breaking

LEARNING MORE

Books

Stuff Matters: Exploring the Marvelous Materials That Shape Our Man-made World by Mark Miodownik, Mariner Books, 2015

Henry Bessemer: Making Steel from Iron by Kathleen Tracy, Mitchell. Lane, 2005

Everything Rocks and Minerals by Steve Tomecek, National Geographic Kids, 2011

Websites

Learn more about the properties of different materials.
www.sciencekids.co.nz/gamesactivities/materialproperties.html

Find out about properties of common materials.
www.bbc.co.uk/bitesize/ks2/science/materials/material_properties/read/1/

Read more about armor and chain mail.
www.ducksters.com/history/middle_ages/knight_armor_and_weapons.php

INDEX